TREY C. ROLAND

Learn iPhone

7

In 15 Minutes

**iPhone 7 user guide with illustrations;
iPhone 7 instruction book
for seniors**

Learn iPhone 7

In 15 Minutes

**iPhone 7 user guide with illustrations;
iPhone 7 instruction book
for seniors**

TREY C. ROLAND

Dedicated to all my readers

Contents

Introduction

This is a guide for new users of the iPhone 8/8 plus.

This book is in three (3) parts. The first part introduces you on how to get started with the iPhone 7/7 pus, the middle exposes a comprehensive list of tricks and how to execute them, while the last part concludes with useful troubleshooting tips.

Also, with the several illustrations, Beginners and Seniors will find learning easier. Now, start savoring the content of this book and become clearly aware of almost all that your iPhone 7 can do. .

PART 1

Insight into the iPhone 7 and iPhone 7 Plus

At first glance, the iPhone 7 and 7 Plus are quite the same as the previous 6s and 6s Plus. You still get the 4.7 screen size for the iPhone 7 and 6s while the Pluses feature a 5.5 screen size. Even then, when you pay close attention to the devices, you are bound to notice visual differences not to mention the massive improvements internally.

You don't find the Antenna bands running along the back of the new devices. And not only do you get the Silver, Rose Gold and Gold colors, Apple also released the Black color for those looking for a matte look. For a high gloss aesthetic, Apple provides the Jet Black.

The camera at the back also protrudes more and you would even notice this more on the iPhone 7 Plus since it features a dual-camera. The bottom of the device has also changed as the headphone jack was removed. That area is now occupied by another speaker hole. The only extra hole on the left is for the microphone.

This is a bummer for those with really expensive 3.5mm cord headphones. While you can decide to buy a wireless headphone so that you could connect through Bluetooth, you would also do well to check out the Lightning to Headphone adapter. Word is that Apple is no longer including this in the box but you can easily find some really quality ones from Belkin. This works by connecting your wired headphones to the adapter and connecting the adapter to the iPhone through Lightning. Nice and easy, except for the fact that you could easily forget to carry this adapter with you.

The iPhone 7 and 7 Plus body has also been revamped to feature a 1P67 water and dust resistance. This means that your iPhone device will be able to withstand rain and water splashes. And even when it gets submerged in water, your iPhone device would still be okay; though you would want to take it out quickly.

Then again, the iPhone 7 doesn't feature a 'real' home button. All you have there is a disc made to look like a button but it's a pressure sensitive one that only requires you to tap. It's linked to the Taptic touch feature that gives you haptic feedback so that you feel like you're pressing a button. It's just like the feeling you get with new Macs

Haptic feedbacks are just vibrations received when you do some actions like making a payment with Apple Pay or unlocking the device. The vibration is to let you know that those actions are successful. With the home button, you don't experience the click of a real button, instead, you feel these vibrations

But the great part of this haptic feedback is that you can choose how intense the feedback is. You can choose to make it very strong so that you really notice that your commands have been recognized or you could make it light so that you barely notice something vibrated. Most would like to settle for middle but do what seems best to you.

You should know, though, that the home button of the iPhone 7 is capacitive. Meaning, it needs contact with skin or some kind of capacitive object to work. If you don't use these, then your touch won't be registered. This is not like the home button of previous generation devices, but it's because those home buttons are physical.

Another feature of the iPhone 7 home button is the Touch ID sensor. If you don't know what Touch ID is, it's a fingerprint detector that unlocks the device when your own fingerprint gets in touch with the home button. With this, you don't need passwords or passcodes since Touch ID gives top security for payments made with Apple Pay and other functions

The display on the iPhone 7 also gets brighter than the iPhone 6s by about 25%. What this means is that when you are outdoors in full sunlight, the brighter screen will enable you to see without squinting your eyes. The colors on the screen are also more saturated and vibrant thanks to the cinema wide color range and color management

The iPhone 7 screen resolution is 1134 x 750 with 326ppi while the iPhone 7 Plus resolution is 1920 x 1080 with 401ppi. While you get quality screen resolution, it's all still fitted within the 4.7 and 5.5 inches display size of the iPhone 7 and iPhone 7 Plus. But the high contrast rating and peak brightness of the iPhone 7 are not the only cool things about this device.

You also get to experience the goodness of 3D Touch. 3D Touch is still a very essential feature of the iPhone display and it's etched into the layers of the screen. But for the iPhone 7 and Plus, 3D Touch is an extended feature that gives the iPhone the ability to recognize the pressure level and act according to the pressure. This is why a light tap doesn't give the same results as force pressing.

With the iOS 9 and 10, 3D Touch allows you to use the Pop and Peek gestures and it's not only for the home screen, it works great also for iOS applications. To Peek, you just do a light press while force pressing will awaken the Pop feature. They do different things but they are basically meant for getting more of menus and using an app without actually opening it.

Another feature worth mentioning about the iPhone 7 is the camera. The iPhone 7 and 7 Plus cameras are a huge leap in the making of mobile cameras. With these, you get photos that are actually sharper, brighter and clearer – this quality doesn't change even in low lighting conditions.

While the features of the iPhone 7 camera are embedded in the iPhone 7 Plus, the Plus has an upper hand. The iPhone 7 Plus has a second camera – a 12 MP telephoto 56mm lens with an aperture f/2,8. The extra camera basically allows users to get zoomed in shots and still get super quality.

iPhone 7 setup

When you turn on either the iPhone 7 or the iPhone 7 Plus, you will be welcomed by the Hello screen. From there on, you have your Setup wizard to help you in setting up your device. But before you even turn on the new iPhone, you need to do some setting up with the old iPhone. But this will totally depend on how you want to start the iPhone 7

You need to know the options you have. There are 3 main ways you can start with your new iPhone. You can either choose to **Set Up as New** to **Restore a Backup from a previous iPhone** or to **Import Data from Android**.

When it comes to setting up as new, it basically means that you are using the iPhone 7 from scratch. People who get the iPhone 7 as their first smartphone or who just want to leave old things behind would want to select this option.

You can restore a backup from a previous iPhone depending on the service you backed up with. You can basically back up with either iTunes using a USB cable or over Wi-Fi via iCloud. If your previous device was an iOS device, then this option is for you. The import from Android option is for those with an Android device. Now, there's an app in Google Play from Apple that allows you to move data from the phone over to your new device.

But the process of setting up the iPhone at the first stage is the same whether you are restoring backup or setting up as new.

1. Turn on the iPhone 7 and swipe on the screen to start setting up the device
2. Choose your language. Depending on where you bought your iPhone, this option should automatically pick your home country
3. Select your region or your country. This also should be set to the region you live depending on where you bought it. But feel free to make another selection
4. Choose a Wi-Fi network and input a password when required. You can decide to

set this up now or later. If you don't have a Wi-Fi connection available, you can choose the option to use **Cellular**.

5. You may have to wait for some time to activate your iPhone 7. Most times, it shouldn't be more than some seconds for your device to get activated.

6. Choose the option to **Enable Location Service**. Not everyone will be okay with Apple tracking their location through GPS so you can choose to **Skip Locations Services**. But do keep in mind that not enabling Location Services won't allow you to use services requiring your location like getting restaurants nearby or using Maps. But nothing is set on stone so you can set it up later if you ever change your mind

7. Set up the Touch ID feature and passcode. If you don't want to start all that now, you

can choose **Set Up Touch ID Later**. But it doesn't matter if you skipped setting up Touch ID when setting up your device, make sure you set it up as it is important. As a result of its top security, no one can access your iPhone except you

8. You would then to be given the option either to **Restore a Backup, Import from Android** or to **Set Up as New**

Apps & Data

Restore from iCloud Backup

Restore from iTunes Backup

Set Up as New iPhone

Move Data from Android

What does restoring do?

Your personal data and purchased
content will appear on your device,
automatically.

How to move data to a new iPhone

When you get to the **Apps and Data** screen that

gives you the option to Restore or Set up as New,

you would need to have a backup first before you

choose the option to Restore a Backup. Here's

how you use iCloud to back up first then restore
to your new iPhone

1. On your old iPhone enter the **Settings**

2. Hit the banner for **Apple ID** at the top

3. Choose **iCloud**, then **iCloud Backup**

4. Select **Back Up Now**

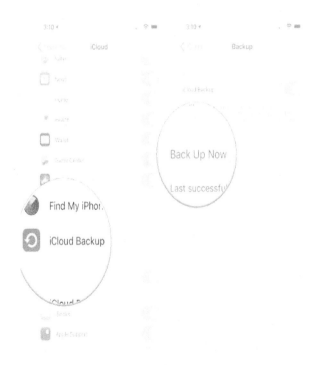

5. You will need to give the iPhone sometime to back up completely. When it's done, turn off the iPhone and take out the SIM card.

6. Insert the SIM card into your new iPhone 7 or iPhone 7 Plus and turn it on.

7. Go through with the directions to set up your iPhone and choose **Restore from iCloud Backup** when you reach the **Apps and Data** screen

●●● Verizon 📶 2:10 PM ▰▰ ·

‹

Apps & Data

Restore from iCloud Backup

Restore from iTunes Backup

Set Up as New iPhone

Move Data from Android

What does restoring do?

Your personal data and purchased
content will appear on your device,
automatically.

8. You will be asked to log in to your iCloud account, enter your details. Choose **Next**

9. Then **Agree**

10. Select the backup you just created.

If you would like to use iTunes,

1. Connect your old iPhone to your computer via USB

2. Open **iTunes** and hit the **device icon**

3. Choose **Encrypt Backup** and choose a password. You only need to add a password if you choose this Encrypt Backup option for the first time.

4. Select **Back Up Now**

5. When backup is complete, disconnect your iPhone. Connect your new iPhone 7 to your computer.

6. Start up your new iPhone and begin setting up all the way to the **Apps and Data** screen

7. Choose to **Restore iTunes Backup**

8. Choose **Restore from This Backup** on your computer. Select the backup you just made

9. Choose **Continue**

10. You will be asked to input the Encrypt Backup password you just added.

Be sure not to disconnect your iPhone until restoration is complete.

To set up as new

1. Sign in to your iCloud account. You only enter your Apple ID and password. You can also choose to **Create a New Apple ID**.

2. Choose to **Agree** to the Terms and Conditions

3. Choose to **Set up Apple Pay** and **iCloud Keychain**. iCloud Keychain will save your passwords and synchronize them across your devices.

4. When the option comes for Siri, Set it up.

5. For the times when issues will arise or apps will crash, choose to **Send Diagnostic Information** to Apple. If you would not like to enable this, select **Don't Send**

6. If you would like to have the texts and icons larger, choose the **Display Zoom** option

PART 2

Tips and Tricks for the iPhone 7 and iPhone 7 Plus

The new iPhone 7 home button

While there's the absence of the headphone jack on your iPhone 7, one of the changes you will easily spot on the iPhone 7 is the new home button. This new home button does not move or press like the one on previous generation iPhones.

The new home button is just like a circular trackpad that only requires you to tap. With the help of haptic feedback, the home button gives you that button like feel. But it's a good thing Apple allows its users to change the way the home button feels on the iPhone 7 and iPhone 7 Plus.

You can set it to 3 feedback levels and select the one that suits you the most. If you want to adjust the home button of the iPhone 7 and iPhone 7 Plus device, these are the steps

1. Enter the **Settings** on the iPhone

2. Select **Home Button**

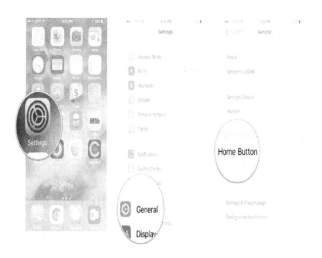

3. Test out the different feedbacks. When you choose a level you like, tap **Done**

New way to restart the device

Since the iPhone 7 home button isn't the movable type anymore but it's fixed in one spot, the way you force restart the iPhone will change. With iPhones before the iPhone 7, you could easily hit the **Power** button and the home button at the same time to force restart the iPhone.

If you try that approach with the iPhone 7 when the device freezes, it won't force restart. Apple has set another button combo to summon the force restart action with their new phones. To force restart on the iPhone 7 or iPhone 7 Plus

1. Press and hold the **Power** button. It's the button at the side of the device
2. Press and hold down the **Volume Down** button simultaneously.

3. Don't release your hold until the iPhone shows the Apple screen to restart

Optical zoom on the iPhone

The latest iPhone series have dual (or even triple) cameras at the rear. One of these is used for 2x optical zoom. And it's a very excellent option to use optical zoom on the iPhone 7 Plus.

This kind of zooming works different for a regular iPhone. For that, you just need to zoom in normally with the pinch gesture. If you are wondering how to use this 2x optical zoom feature on the iPhone 7 Plus, here's how

1. Fire up the **Camera** app on the iPhone. You could slide to the camera if you are on the lock screen
2. Enter the **Photo** mode. By default, the camera should be set to Photo but if it is in Square or Video, slide to change to Photo

3. Just over the yellow **Photo** icon, you should see the 1x option in circle. Tap this

4. After you tap the 1x, the camera should zoom in closer to the object and the number would become 2x.

5. That's the optical zoom feature, hit shutter to take your photos. If you want to go back to the standard 1x, just hit the 2x icon.

Before you can take photos with the 2x telephoto lens, you would need to have an iPhone with a dual camera setup.

You should also take note that the 2x optical zoom is very different from digital zoom. Digital zoom is the type of zoom that requires you to expand the screen with your fingers. Optical zoom on the other hand, just requires that you tap the 1x.

While they both have the word 'zoom' in their name, they are very different features. You always want to use optical zoom. The reason is that optical zoom makes use of the iPhone's camera lens to bring the subject nearer to the camera. You will need the second 2x camera on the Plus model for this.

Digital zoom, on the other hand, can be done with any camera but the results are very mediocre (if not pitiful). This is because digital zoom only enlarges what you see on the screen. No camera technology is required to bring the subject closer; it just zooms in on the photo on the screen. The result of this is a very low-quality and pixelated photo

New feature to lock the zoom

The zooming abilities of the new iPhones have undoubtedly increased. As a result, there's a new setting in the Camera settings that allows you to lock the lens when you shoot a video. If you are one who records videos a lot, you will notice that the iPhone can easily switch from the wide-angle lens to the telephoto lens.

And that's not the only disadvantage. When this happens, the image flickers as the video is being recorded thereby disrupting your shot. But now all you have to do is to

1. Enter the **Settings**

2. Choose **Photos & Camera**

3. Select **Record Video**

4. When you see the option for **Lock Camera Lens**, turn it on.

Rest finger to open on the iPhone 7

When iOS 10 was introduced, it brought new features with it. Some were really great, others, a bit unnecessary. But one of the problems that the iOS helped to solve was pressing the home button to unlock the device. It wasn't a big deal but why do you need to press a button all the way down just unlock.

Why press when you could just tap the home button like Android users. It's a little step but it would be a lifesaver if it could be avoided. If you share the same sentiment and you don't like pressing the home button, well, aren't you the fortunate one?

Apple provided the Rest Finger To Open feature just for that.

1. Enter the **Settings**

2. Choose **General**

3. Select **Accessibility**

4. Hit **Home Button**

5. Then turn on the option for **Rest Finger To Open**

From here on, you do not need to press the home button when you want to unlock the device. All you need to do is to make sure your finger comes in contact with the button and you're good. A small step, but it's saving lives.

Access camera from the lock screen

With the iOS 10 on the iPhone 7, the camera shortcut also changed. It used to be at the lower corner of the lock screen. Does this mean that you can no longer open the camera from the lock screen? No, that feature is just too useful to be taken out.

Now, all you have to do when you are on the iOS 10 lock screen is to slide to the left and the Camera app will be opened easily. So you do not have to swipe up, you swipe left. You may not spot this easily because of the background image on the lock screen, but there are 3 little icons at the bottom of the screen. Among these 3 is the Camera icon.

Since swiping to the left summons the camera, swiping to the right brings up the Today's view screen. From here, you can see widgets information like the weather app and other mini apps as well as appointments on your calendar. You can also choose to edit this widget list by selecting the button for **Edit**.

Why not use the trackpad

Thanks to 3D Touch, you can transform your iPhone's keyboard to a trackpad. While this feature isn't new to the iPhone, it's a really cool one you want to try out. So if you ever need to type an email, note, comment or message and you would like to slide the cursor to select a word and correct an error, you could use the trackpad feature and easily make your edit.

Without this trackpad feature, you would need to use your large thumb to tap the word or area you want to edit so that the cursor can appear there. But that method isn't very precise and because your finger is obstructing your view, you can't see where the cursor is. It would take a couple of taps before you actually get it right.

Instead, use the trackpad feature by pressing hard on the keyboard. The keys will vanish and you'll be greeted with a trackpad like that on your Mac. All you have to do now is to swipe your finger to move the cursor. Control the cursor to get to the area that needs correction. To select the word, you can just hard press again. If you hard press 2 times, the entire sentence is selected.

The Today's Screen

The Today's Screen is available on the iOS 10 and you can easily access it on the lock screen. But it comes with a new look and appearance on your iPhone 7. Nevertheless, you'll want to do some customizations to make it yours when you start using your iPhone device.

When you are on the home screen or lock screen, slide right to bring up the Today's Screen. If you haven't tampered with this screen, you should be seeing widgets telling you the conditions of the weather, calendar events, news headlines, destinations for Maps and Siri recommendations.

It's a cool view, but you could do better.

1. Move down to the lower part of the Today's Screen

2. Choose **Edit** to change the view of the screen

3. You can add more widgets or delete needless ones

4. You are not stuck with Apple's app widgets, if you have a third-party app installed, you should also be able to add its widget. You can find the option in the segment for **More Widgets**

 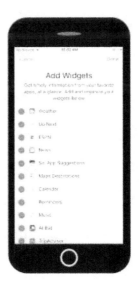

You can drown the iPhone but be careful

The iPhone 7 and iPhone 7 Plus have both been upgraded to hold up against water splashes. The new iPhones are said to have a resistance rating of IP67. This means that if your phone gets dropped into a body of water for about 30 min and as deep as 3 feet (1 meter), it would still come out without any defect.

The iPhone can resist water in a way that older devices cannot. The iPhone 7 was even tested to prove this fact; water was spilled on the iPhone and it was fine. It was then pitched into a cup of water and nothing unpleasant resulted.

Nevertheless, you don't want to rely too much on this brand-new superpower of water resistance. If your iPhone ever drops into water, make sure you wipe your phone dry before you use it again. And most importantly, do not charge until your iPhone is dry.

To help with this, Apple built a feature into the iPhone 7 that will alert you when the iPhone is moist. When you see this warning, remove the iPhone from charger very quickly and turn off the iPhone. Leave it to dry out before powering on.

Live Photos

The idea of shooting Live Photos began with the iPhone 6s. Live Photos are basically images that are animated and you can shoot these with the camera of your iPhone. These images become animated because the camera starts to record some seconds before you take the photo and some seconds after.

But if you are coming from older iPhones, you may need an update on how to snap with the Live Photos feature. The Live Photos feature is turned on by default but to know if it's enabled or not, you should see the bulls eye sign just on top the camera viewfinder. If this icon is turned on, it will be yellow.

Tap this icon to turn on Live Photos. The camera starts to record 1.5 seconds before you tap shutter and 1.5 seconds after. And you don't only get video, sound is also recorded. During the 1.5 seconds after you tap shutter, you should see **LIVE** show up to let you know that the camera is still shooting the Live Photo. If you put down the camera before the **LIVE** vanishes, your photos will be blurry.

Turn off the touch feedback

The Taptic engine got a huge increase in the iPhone 7 and iPhone 7 Plus. If you do not know what the Taptic engine is, it's the engine responsible for creating vibrations on the smartphone. Since the iPhone 7 has more accurate abilities, Apple added the touch feedback technology in the operating system.

That's the reason why almost every action is accompanied by a feedback. Anytime you spin a dial, you feel this touch feedback, the same goes for deleting emails in Mail by swiping, sliding down the Notification and a lot more.

While the buzzes and vibrations are exciting at first, they can become very distracting. And it's a good thing Apple added the deactivate button

1. Enter the **Settings**

2. Move to the new option for **Sounds & Haptics**.

3. Move down to the bottom of the list and select the **System Haptics**

4. Turn it off

5. From now, you won't get disturbed by those blips and vibrations.

Deactivate messages effects

With the iOS 10 came one of the biggest brand new features; the option to improve your messages by sending texts with different effects. You can send messages with bubble and flashy effects to give your messages more substance and feel.

But these effects aren't for everyone. It could be that you are not the touchy-feely type to care about such sparkly effects or you don't like motion on the screen, whatever the case, you can turn them off easily. This way, you don't have to experience confetti or balloons coming your way when it's time for congratulations.

1. Enter the **Settings**
2. Choose **General**
3. Select **Accessibility**
4. Then **Reduce Motion**. Enable this feature

Take note, though, that this Reduce motion option will not only stop the messages effects, it would virtually limit all effects on the operating system that are motion based.

On the other hand, if you are racking your brain because you are not able to use message effects for your texts, chances are someone already turned on the Reduce motion feature. Follow the steps above to enable it again.

Use 4k on the iPhone 7

The camera at the back of your iPhone can shoot quality HD videos and that's cool. But here's something cooler? You can also shoot videos at 4k resolution on the iPhone? The iPhone can also let you edit the fps or frames per second in your videos. The result of a high fps and 4k would give you a seamless video with very high quality.

But the iPhone 7 isn't the first iPhone to record videos in 4k. The iPhone 6 started this so if you have the iPhone 6 that's on iOS 9 or higher, you can use this supercharged camera shooting upgrade.

But the process of shooting in 4k is not as easy as entering the camera app and hitting the shutter button. You have to do some digging, but you don't have to panic, it's really easy to do.

1. Fire up the **Settings** app
2. Select **Camera**
3. Choose **Record Video**
4. From the option showed on the screen, choose your resolution

While you would enjoy shooting and watching videos in 4k, you want to remember that with a high resolution comes a bigger file size. Like for example, shooting videos with 4k at 60 fps gives you 400 MB for every minute; so a 30-minute video would bring tragedy to your storage. If you were shooting Slo-Mo, the highest is 1080p at 240fps and a minute video would be 480 MB

Color filters

It doesn't matter if the screen of the iPhone 7 is configured to be at its brightest, you won't find it easy to navigate the device if you experience some kind of color blindness. But the iOS 10 on the iPhone can assist; it adds different types of new filter selections to help if you don't find it easy telling colors apart. To use this,

1. Enter the **Settings** app

2. Choose **General**

3. Select **Accessibility**

4. Then **Display Accommodations**

5. Tap **Color Filters**.

6. When you get to this screen, you can select from different options. You can choose a filter for **Green/Red**, **Red/Green**, **Blue/Yellow** or even **Grayscale**.

These color filters can assist anyone dealing with Deuteranopia, Protanopia or Tritanopia. If these filters don't do much to help out, you can also tint the colors of the entire screen. It could be helpful to select an intensity or hue for the display.

You would see color illustrations shown on the screen to help understand how a filter would look.

Wipe out all notifications on the iPhone with 3D Touch

Don't we all loathe having the screen of the iPhone loaded with messages, apps and call notifications. While it doesn't take years to clear these one by one, iOS 10 brought a feature to the iPhone 7 that allows you to wipe out all the notifications on the screen at once.

For this 'clear all notifications at once' trick to work, your iPhone needs to have a 3D Touch screen. And what do you know? The iPhone 7 does! If the iPhone isn't iPhone 6s or higher, it won't work. Here's how you do it

1. From the top of the screen, swipe down to show the Notifications center

2. Apply 3D Touch by force pressing the **X** button on top the notifications list

3. The **Clear All Notifications** button should show up, select this

4. Notifications are cleared instantaneously

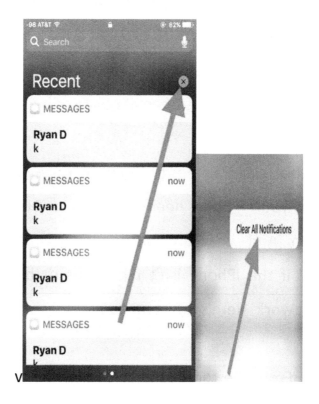

This lovely feature came from the Apple Watch which also allows you to hard press the screen to clear all notifications. It would be a shame, really, if the iPhone was left out on this superb feature. For the devices without 3D Touch, you'll need to use the **Clear** option to clear the notifications. But you'll have to do it continuously for each section almost every time.

Don't strain, magnify

For those with some kind of visual impairment, the iPhone 7 comes with a handy feature in the accessibility settings. In fact, you would even find this helpful if you are not just in the mood to strain your eyes to read a text in small print. This can be a struggle, especially in poor lighting conditions.

This feature is called Magnifier and before you roll your eyes and say that this is the same as firing up the camera and zooming in, it's not. It's way more than that, it's a separate feature meant to be used to take a look at something far away or in small print. And it's very easy to activate this feature

1. Launch the **Settings**
2. Move to **General**
3. Tap **Accessibility**

4. Choose **Magnifier**

5. Then turn on the toggle for **Magnifier**

When you've enabled this magnifier, all you have to do is click the home button 3 times and it will come up. Another cool way to bring this feature closer to you is to add it to the Control Center.

1. Enter the **Settings**

2. Then **Control Center**

3. Select **Customize Controls**

4. Add **Magnifier**

When you summon the magnifier, you'll be presented with a camera viewfinder. Again, this is not your regular camera app because it has some features made exclusively for it. Like you have the yellow slider just below the viewfinder for magnifying the scene. You'll also find the button for Flashlight. It's helpful for those lowlight scenes when you need some illumination.

The shutter-like button at the center doesn't take any picture. It only freezes what you see on the screen. When the image is frozen, you will see a yellow ring surrounding the button. With this, you don't need to point at the image, you can move the phone freely and the photo would still be frozen on the screen.

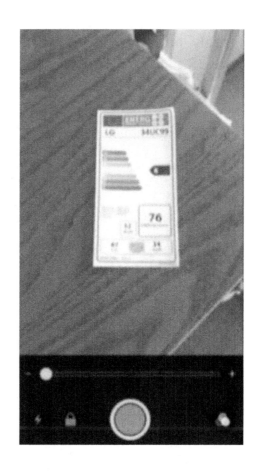

ENERGY ENERGIE
ENERGI

52
Wat

87

Save Image | Share

2010/1062 · 2017

You can still use the yellow slider to magnify the image while it's frozen. A frozen image doesn't save to Camera Roll, it just stays unmoving on the screen. But if you love the shot to the extent you'll want to save it, press and hold the image. Choose **Save Image** from the menu. Do you want to show the image to your friends? Use the **Share** option on the same menu.

Shortcuts on the Control Center

We really don't know what we'd do without the Control Center on the iPhone. It just brings a lot of features closer and you can easily access it by sliding up from the bottom of the display. But now on the iOS 10, not only do you get easy access to your favorite features like Calculator, Timer, Camera and Flashlight but you can also get more options for them.

This is made possible with 3D Touch that allows you to hard press a feature on the Control Center to summon extra options. As a result of this, you could even increase the intensity of the Flashlight. Simply force press on the Flashlight in the Control Center and you'll be able to choose between low, medium and bright.

If you force press the Timer, you can start a timer for a set duration like 1 minute, 5 minutes, 1 hour and so on. Force pressing the Calculator icon would allow you to copy the previous calculation while the Camera icon would make you choose between, Video, Selfie, Slow-Mo or the normal Photo modes.

Add next song to queue

Once again, the Music app got a renovation with iOS 10 and this new version is equipped with a dozen features that you can access easily with 3D Touch on the iPhone 7. With 3D Touch, you literally don't have to open an app before you make a selection.

One of the more amazing features in the Music app is the incorporation of Up Next. So if you are listening to a song but you immediately remember a song you'll like to play next, you could just look for the track in the app and hard press it. You will be shown a couple of useful options to add the track to a playlist, love the track, remove download, share the song or to dislike the track.

To add the song to your Up Next queue, simply select the **Play Next** option. And all of this works without removing your finger from the display. Don't stop at tracks, try this feature with playlists and albums too.

Use Maps to get weather reports

If you're heading out and you're wondering about the weather situation in the place you are headed, you don't have to look any further than Maps to check a forecast. And thanks to 3D Touch on the iPhone 7 and iPhone 7 Plus, you can get more options.

With this, a 7-hour forecast can be shown when you press on the temperature option. If you continue to press, you will be invited to the in-built Weather app to get the location's full forecast.

Control media playback

On iOS 10, the Control Center was revamped. You can still access your favorite features from here but you get more room for items and icons are larger. If you don't know your way around things, you would immediately start looking for your media controls.

The way the Control Center works is by showing panes. So there's another **Now Playing** card containing your media controls. If you want to see these controls

1. Swipe up to reveal the Control Center
2. Swipe left when the Control Center is opened
3. You'll be shown your play, next and previous playback options here. The volume slider is also included

It's not only the media controls that got changed, the controls for audio and video also got a redesign. Now the control for video and audio are separated. Like for example, turning on AirPlay mirroring for your Apple TV on the first pane will have you pressing the button for AirPlay.

But for switching to Bluetooth headset from the iPhone speakers, you need to choose the Headphones icon on the second pane.

New way to switch between apps

Many of us are aware of the quick function to switch between apps by clicking the home button twice and selecting the app from the multitasking display. That method was helpful and quick but if you have got a 3D Touch phone, you'll want to do better than that.

Those who use 3D Touch devices have an upper hand in reaching recently used apps. With this, you don't have to bother about double tapping the home button and choosing your recently used apps. In fact, you wouldn't even need to press the little **Back To ...** button that appears at the top of almost every app.

To move back to a recently used app on your iPhone 7 and iPhone 7 Plus with 3D Touch,

1. Force press the screen's left edge.
2. You can hold that press for a while and the multitasking screen would come up.
3. On the other hand, if you slide to the right and release your hold, you'll be brought to the app switcher where you can open any of your previously used apps.

To know the right time to swipe right, you'll have to wait for the 3D Touch Taptic feedback to come on. If you don't get this feedback and you swipe, you could start to scroll up in the app you were in. It could take a while to get used to but in time, it'll be second nature.

It's almost the same as the 'double press home button' method but some would argue it's easier.

Whatever the case, it's always nice to have more than 1 method to solve a problem. And nowadays, when app switching is a huge time saver, it does no harm having 3 ways to do it

Using Apple Pay

It has taken some time but the option to use tap and pay is now becoming a thing. Now, you don't need to carry your card everywhere to swipe or fix in a reader. Using card skimmers is already becoming a thing of the past.

You can tap to pay for your coffee, rides on a public bus, or for groceries and it's all thanks to Apple Pay. If you are upgrading to the iPhone 7 from any iPhone before iPhone 6, this would be your first step into the Apple Pay world. While the latest iPhones make use of Face ID to authorize a payment, the iPhone 7 and 7 Plus only need Touch ID or a passcode.

If a terminal uses Near Field communications, you can tap your iPhone and pay. Most time, stores that support Apple Pay would have the Apple Pay logo. But the big question now is; how do you set up Apple Pay on your iPhone? We'll show you how, I mean, that's what we're here for.

 Back

Add Card

Enter your security code for your card on file with iTunes or App Store.

Card Number   VISA

1. If you want to set up Apple Pay on your iPhone 7 or iPhone 7 Plus, you would have to upgrade to the latest iOS version. You can check your iOS version by
   - Entering the **Settings**
   - Choosing **General**
   - Then **Software Update**

- Make sure you are logged into iCloud

2. To begin the setup, fire up the **Wallet** app

3. Touch the **plus** sign at the upper right or the **Add Card** option

4. You can choose to scan a debit card or credit card. This will upload all the appropriate details. You can also choose to enter your information manually.

5. Depending on the bank you use, instructions for authorization should be sent to you. Do check your messages or emails to see if you received any additional directions.

6. After your bank has accepted the card to be used for Apple Pay, select the **Next** option

7. To use Apple Pay, you need to add at least 1 card to the Wallet app which you've already done successfully. Enter the Settings and make whatever changes are necessary

- **Settings**

- Then **Wallet & Apple Pay**.

From here, you can set the card used to make purchases by default. You can also set the card used for transit. Depending on your preferences, you can also choose to enable Apple Pay Cash

That all nice and good but how do you use Apple Pay to pay for stuff in stores.

1. Place your device close to the contactless card reader and you should see the photo of your card show up on the screen.

2. At this point, you'll place your finger on the sensor for Touch ID (the home button). But do not press it. After a second or two, it should approve your fingerprint and you'll be good to go. The process would be a tad different if you were using a Face ID iPhone.

3. If you would like to use another card, touch the card shown on the screen and select the other card. A setting many love to enable is the setting to prepare a card from the lock screen then summon it by clicking the home button twice.

Using Apple Pay on the iPhone X, XS, XS Max, 11, 11 Pro and 11 Pro Max is a bit different since these device are not equipped with Touch ID fingerprint sensors. Rather, you'll have to look at the iPhone camera to authenticate with Face ID. Other than that, it's pretty much the same process.

But another question is; is it safe?

Contactless payments with Apple Pay are safe in general. And since you'll be using Touch ID or a passcode to authenticate, the system is a lot safer. If you plan on traveling to another country soon, it is recommended you enable Apple Pay on your iPhone before you leave.

If contactless payment is available in that country, you should take some time to master Apple Pay first so when you eventually want to make a payment there, you'll be doing so like a local.

View your iCloud storage easily

There are many emails, files and photos hidden in your iCloud and if you are wondering how many they are, you can find them in the settings

1. Enter the **Settings**
2. Touch your Apple ID at the upper part of the display
3. Choose **iCloud**
4. From this screen, you will be able to see the usage of your iCloud storage. You can tap this to find out how much space is left.

If you don't have enough storage space, you do well to delete a few things to create room. But if you are so attached to your files to the extent that you can't bear to see one go, you could just purchase more iCloud storage

Editing your Live Photo

When you take a Live Photo on the iPhone 7 or iPhone 7 Plus, you now have the opportunity to edit it and give it a better look. The feature to tweak Live Photos with the Photos app came in iOS 10. To do this

1. Enter the **Photos** app and select the Live Photo you want to edit

2. Select the button for **Edit** at the bottom

3. You would find the option to straighten, crop or to fine-tune color and lighting. You could also add a filter to the Live Photo without making it a static photo.

This option makes Live Photos more like normal photos and since edits done on normal photos are non-destructive (not permanent), you can also go back many steps on your Live Photo edits

Raise To Wake on the iPhone 7 and 7 Plus

If you thought that the Rest Finger To Open feature was fast enough, think again, iOS 10 makes Raise To Wake available. The Raise To Wake feature causes the screen of the iPhone to come on immediately you pick it up and we would add that this feature could just be the best thing included in the iOS

But not everyone loves this feature and you may like it better for your iPhone to come to life only when you touch a button. If that's the case, disabling Raise To Wake is merely a tap away.

1. Enter the **Settings**, of course
2. Choose the option for **Display & Brightness**
3. You would find the section where you can change the time for the phone's Auto-Lock

feature. Just beneath that, there's a toggle that gives you the option to disable **Raise To Wake**

On the other hand, if you are interested in Raise To Wake and you're wondering why it's not working on your iPhone, it could be that you've disabled it by mistake. Follow the directions above to turn it on again.

Toggling off Auto Brightness

If you don't like your iPhone adjusting the brightness of the screen by itself, then there's a chance that you've disabled Auto Brightness at one time or the other. In the past, it was easy to do and your instincts would lead you to enter the **Display and Brightness** settings to disable it.

But it's a dead end now. If you ever upgrade to iOS 11 or higher, Display and Brightness still deals with all things related to the iPhone's display and brightness except the Auto Brightness function. It seems Apple wants us to dig further to get this setting and for some reason best known to them, they've stashed it away in the Accessibility setting.

So to reach the Auto Brightness setting

1. Enter the **Settings**
2. Choose **Accessibility**
3. Then **Display Accommodations**

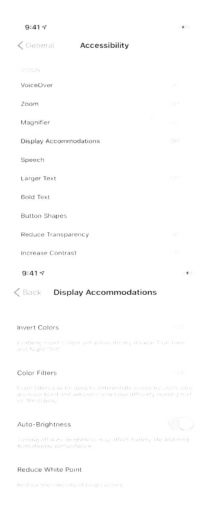

4. Turn on the toggle for **Auto Brightness**

Taking a screenshot

If you would like to take a screenshot on the iPhone 7, hold down the **Power** button and the home button simultaneously. When the screenshot is taken, a preview should show up at the lower corner. But it would vanish after about 5 seconds so if you want to edit it tap the preview before it goes away.

But you can skip the 5 seconds and dismiss the preview by swiping it to the left. When you are done with editing the screenshot, select **Done** to save. All screenshots would be automatically sent to Camera Roll

How to start Emergency SOS

No one indeed wants to be in a dreadful situation but if something terrible ever happens and you need to call emergency services, you could do so easily by hitting the **Power** button 5 times very quickly. When the Emergency SOS slider shows up, slide across and you would be able to call emergency services right away.

When you do this, your present location would also be sent to your emergency contacts when you are done with the call. Also, the Touch ID feature would also be locked. The thinking behind this is that, you won't be forced to paste your fingerprint when you don't want to.

Live without the headphone jack

Since the headphone jack was displaced by Apple in the iPhone 7 and 7 Plus devices, they included a Lightning adapter in the iPhone box so that you can still listen to music with any headphones making use of the 3.5mm jack. Since many headphones don't use the Lightning connector, this adapter would prove useful.

But you could get caught in the excitement of getting a new iPhone that you would not see the adapter. You should find it after removing the EarPods. Apple is showing signs of stopping the addition of this adapter in the box so if you don't find yours, have a look at Belkin's adapter collection

Music and charging simultaneously

On the other hand, if your headphones are those with a Lightning connector and you're listening to music while the battery is blinking 1%, what do you do? The normal step to take is to rip out the headphones and plug in the charger.

But you don't have to do that with Belkin's double Lightning connector. So you can use one to listen to audio while you charge with the other.

PART 3

IPhone 7 and iPhone 7 Plus Troubleshooting

A first look at the iPhone 7 and you'd almost call it the iPhone 6s, but a little more examination of the device and you'll find that there are a lot of improvements. If nothing the camera is top notch, you get dual speakers and an even higher water resistance rating.

But with these sweet features, the device is not free of hitches and glitches. You will run into some form of problem with the device whether small or large. But not too worry, we have here some workarounds and solutions to take away the anxiety

No service on the iPhone

A website made a report on September 2017 about the document from Apple letting us know that the problem of no cellular service on the iPhone 7 is being handled. It was said that Apple has worked out a solution for the problem but for those experiencing it, they released a repair program. While only a small amount of iPhone had this issue, you get a free repair at an Apple store if your phone is

eligible.

Solution

1. Do check out the repair program at *www.apple.com/support/iphone-7-no-service*

2. Make sure that you have upgraded to the latest iOS version.

3. Take out your SIM card. When you remove the SIM card, return it back to the tray and insert it in the device.

4. Update carrier settings

   - Enter **Settings**

   - Then **General**

   - Choose **About**

   - If you find an update available, update carrier settings

5. Reset network settings

   - Move to the **Settings**

   - Then **General**

   - Choose **Reset**

   - Tap **Reset Network Settings**

6. If nothing happens and problem continues, you may have to reach out to Apple to get a free repair. Eligible devices are A779, A1780 and A1660.

The button for speaker is disabled when making calls

A few users of the iPhone 7 and 7 Plus have said that the speaker button is disabled when receiving or making calls. While the problem only affects a small percentage of people, Apple has acknowledged awareness of the issue. But the company isn't giving free repairs for speakers that don't work again.

Solution

1. A reason for this problem could be that there are some devices paired through Bluetooth to your iPhone. If this is the case, you would need to disable Bluetooth. Swipe up from the bottom and touch Bluetooth to turn it off.

Issues with the Bluetooth

1. Turn off Bluetooth and turn it on again
2. Restart device
3. Unpair your iPhone from any Bluetooth device then pair again
4. Reset network settings
5. Upgrade to the latest iOS version
6. Factory reset your iPhone, but make sure you back up first.

Can't find the 3.5mm jack

Apple decided to murder the headphone jack on the iPhone and they seem to be standing by their decision. But while some don't mind this, others are really bothered by it. If you've spent money on getting some really quality headphones that need the 3.5 mm jack to work, it is understandable if you are really pissed.

The next option is to use headphones that you connect to the Lightning port. But that means that you can't listen to music and charge at the same time. This isn't a big issue but here are a few workarounds

1. Apple used to include an adapter in the iPhone 7 box. But if you don't find an

adapter in yours, you could snag some really good ones from Belkin.

2. Consider going wireless. Let's face it, the world of wires is ending. Get some really good wireless headphones you can connect with Bluetooth. And what better ones than AirPods

The battery life is pitiful

Since everything gets better with newer generation phones, the iPhone 6s battery isn't has superb as the iPhone 7. The battery is bigger and the A10 chip makes it all the more efficient. But on many forums the iPhone 7 battery isn't presented as great. There's been a few complaints about massive battery reduction is a short time. iOS 10.2 update brought about even more criticism for the battery

1. Make sure you update to the new iOS version. Battery issues have been resolved
2. Use Low Power Mode to extend battery life if problem continues
   - Slide into the **Settings**
   - Choose **Battery**
   - Enable **Low Power Mode**.

Using Low Power Mode can be a blessing to your battery because it stops 'Hey Siri', automatic downloading, Mail Fetch, visual effects, background app refresh and a few other settings that sip out of your battery life. If you don't want to turn on Low Power Mode, you can disable each of these settings individually

3. Find out if there's an app swallowing the battery power.

   - Fire up the **Settings** app

   - Then **Battery**

   - Choose **Battery Usage**

   When you find the app, try updating it. If it continues its nuisance, simply uninstall it.

Haptic feedback is not working for 3D Touch

If you notice that the iPhone doesn't give you feedback when you use 3D Touch, know that it is most certainly a bug at work

1. The one thing that seems to work every time is restarting the phone. Haptic feedback should be restored.
2. Turn off and on Haptics
   - Move to the **Settings**
   - Choose **Sounds And Haptics**
   - Turn off and on **System Haptics**

The iPhone refuses to come on

1. Soft reset the iPhone 7 by pressing the **Volume Down** and **Power** button at the same time. If you see the Apple logo it means that your relief has come

2. It could also be that the device has run out of battery. Connect it to a charger

3. Connect it to a Mac or PC and use iTunes to restart the device.

The Phone app continues to crash when using

A lot of iPhone 7 users have said that the Phone app will just lock up or crash when they are in the list for Recent calls, when using the Bluetooth headphones to make calls or when in the settings for the Phone app.

1. Doing the hard or soft rest doesn't seem to solve this case. Try to upgrade to the latest iOS if you haven't

2. If the issue began after you updated the iPhone, it could be that the update wasn't correctly installed. Restore the backup you created before you updated. Then update the phone again.

3. Disabling Exchange contacts was one proposed solution

- Enter the **Settings**

- Then **Contacts**

- Choose **Accounts**

- Select the Exchange account and disable

  Contacts

Mic doesn't work well during calls

This means that the microphone of the iPhone will start to produce some static sounds when you make a call.

1. Do try to restart your device and check if an update is available for your device

2. Back up your iPhone. After backing up, factory reset the device and restore the backup you created.

3. If it's a hardware problem, you'll need to go to an Apple store to get it repaired.

S

The iPhone makes a hissing noise

Many users of the iPhone 7 device have been laying complaints regarding the hissing noise that emanates from the rear of the device. It usually happens when a game or app is working. This simply means that the problem has to do with the processor.

1. Apple didn't give a fix for this issue but you could take back your smartphone and get a replacement. You can contact your carrier or Apple to get a new one.

Device overheating

1. It's very likely that an app is causing this overheating. Be sure to check the apps that were recently updated. If there's a bad update, apps could malfunction thereby resulting in overheating.

2. Factory reset the iPhone after you've backed up

3. If problem continues, do reach out to Apple support.

Not able to activate the iPhone

Many users have said that they always find it a challenge to activate their new iPhone 7. Some may get a message saying that the server for activation is down at the moment. If you receive that, it just means that Apple is trying to manage the amount of people trying to access.

1. It could be because of your cellular connection. If you use celluar to activate the iPhone, try using Wi-Fi.
2. Turn off the iPhone with the **Power** button. When the slider to turn off comes on, drag it. Use the **Power** button to power on the device again.
3. Update iTunes then connect your iPhone to your Mac or PC. Use iTunes to activate your iPhone instead

4. Reach out to your carrier if there have been problems with activating the iPhone 7. You could get a new SIM card.

5. Contact Apple if all efforts prove futile.

Phone call quality is mediocre

If there was a list of the most reported issues of the iPhone 7, this would rank among the top. The Apple forums are full with threads discussing about this problem with the iPhone 7. Some say that the audio coming in is very low or seems like the other person speaking is far way.

1. Try turning the volume up
   - Enter **Settings**
   - Then **Sounds**
   - Use the slider for **Ringer and Alerts** to increase volume
2. If you are finding it hard to hear from the speakers, clear out dust or dirt from the speaker. Make sure that the switch for Ring/Silent is not in silent. Also make sure

that the protective case you use isn't obstructing the speaker.

3. Turn off the iPhone. After a few seconds, turn it back on.

4. Open any app that allows you to play audio. Then increase the volume with the volume keys. You can also use the controls in the Control Center

5. Contact Apple support if you still can't get audio from the speakers

6. Some have said that this issue is common with those using Verizon. Contact the company if that's your carrier

Phone paint peels

1. Apple said that the jet black color is susceptible to scratching and peeling. But their warranty does not cover this damage. Some have opted to sell the phone and get another iPhone in a better color.

3D Touch doesn't function again

3D Touch is one of the killer features of the iPhone 7. You can interact with the screen in an entirely different way and get more menus right from the home screen. But if you find that the feature doesn't work again, you could try these.

1. Turn off the iPhone and turn it back on
2. If you recently plastered a screen protector on the iPhone screen, try taking it off and use 3D Touch without it. If 3D Touch works without the protector, it means that the protector was the source of your misery.
3. Use a cloth to clean the touchscreen. Also make sure your hands are clean

4. It could also be that the 3D Touch feature was disabled either by mistake or your friends
   - Move to **Settings**
   - The **General**
   - Select **Accessibility**
   - Tap **3D Touch** and turn it on if it's off. Also change the sensitivity and see if it works.
5. Contact Apple support or the Apple Store to see if you can get a replacement.

Touch ID doesn't work

On the Apple forums, some have reported to experience problems with Touch ID. It's either the Touch ID feature has trouble working well or it just stops working all together.

1. One of the first things to come to your mind is to restart your iPhone. When the iPhone comes on, use Touch ID and see what happens

2. Use a microfiber cloth to clean your fingers and the Touch ID sensor. It's not uncommon for dirt and dust to hinder the sensor from functioning

3. Make sure you are running the latest iOS version

4. You can also delete fingerprints you've added before then add them again. Scan

many fingers at multiple angles to create several fingerprints

5. If the issue here is that Touch ID doesn't work while charging, try to change the outlet.

6. It could be a hardware issue, contact Apple support at this point.

Disclaimers

This is just an unauthorized iPhone 7/7 plus manual for Beginners and Seniors. It should not be relied upon for learning everything about iPhone 7.

About The Author

Trey Roland has been an active tech researcher for some seven years. His **how-to** guides can be found on reputable tech blogs. He lives with his wife in a small house in Massachusetts.

Printed in Great Britain
by Amazon

83959316R00079